The Human W...
St. Thomas

A Breviary of Philosophy
from
the works of
ST. THOMAS AQUINAS

Arranged by
JOSEF PIEPER

Translated by DROSTAN MacLAREN, O.P.

Must Have Books
503 Deerfield Place
Victoria, BC
V9B 6G5
Canada

ISBN: 9781773238029

Copyright 2021 – Must Have Books

The Human Wisdom of St. Thomas

CONTENTS

CONTENTS

PREFACE

These remarks are not intended to relieve the reader of the necessity of using his mind to get at the meaning of the texts brought together in this Breviary. On the contrary, it seems desirable that the reader should encounter these passages from the works of Thomas Aquinas all on his own and, so to speak, left alone without the aid of an introduction or commentary. It is to be hoped that such an encounter will of itself introduce the reader to the form and design of the whole work of the "Universal Doctor" of Christendom.

The Editor does not wish this book to be read straight through from beginning to end at one sitting, but rather that one or more of these texts, or even a whole section, should be absorbed thoughtfully again and again; in this way the reader will kindle his own thinking, and by gradually making the thought of St. Thomas his own, he will gain some degree of familiarity with the philosophical attitude with which each and every one of these words has been uttered.

I therefore deliberately refrain from even the briefest interpretation of my own of the basic thought of St. Thomas Aquinas contained in this synthesis.

In spite of this, I must not omit to point out that this book, which is intended to be a Breviary of "Philosophy," contains nothing which is Theology in the strict sense of the term. (That can be left over for

a second, similar, self-contained collection of texts.)
Nevertheless, it must be remembered that this philosophy has sprung from the soil of a great theology
in which alone was it able to flourish. Also it can scarcely
remain hidden from anyone who follows the thought
attentively that the reflections here gathered together
lead to the gateway of Theology and Faith. The last
word of our Breviary is that concerning the owl and
the eagle; blessed beyond all human power is a heart
which *like an eagle, flying upwards over the mists of
human frailty, gazes with deeply penetrating eye into
the light of unchangeable truth.*

"Order and Mystery": this title needs a word of
explanation. It has become almost a commonplace
that *ordo* represents a basic category of mediaeval
thought, and especially of the *system* of Thomas
Aquinas.

Ordo: represents the clear and intelligible building
up of reality, as well as the doctrine which reflects that
reality; it represents the satisfaction enjoyed by our
minds in surveying and penetrating the pattern of
life; it represents ways of life which can be trodden
and followed by our thought. And in fact nobody who
has absorbed into himself even a little of the "Summa
Theologica" will be able completely to resist the cold,
logical enchantment which the reason in its search for
enlightenment encounters in an explanation of the
universe constructed with such architectural power.

Nevertheless, anyone who does not see this world,
apparently explained with the utmost clarity of reason,

surrounded on all its borders by pathless mystery does not do justice to Thomas Aquinas.

In the opinion of Thomas, not only does mystery put a limit to the penetrability of reality, but *ordo* itself is interwoven and crossed by mystery. And it is not only mystery in the theological sense, likewise flowing through every part of the whole world, which opposes itself to the grasp of our ordering thought and our attempts at rational mastery. No, the boundary between order and mystery passes through *this* world itself; the effort of human thought, says Thomas, has not been able to track down the essence of a single gnat.

One aim of our Breviary is to demonstrate this double aspect of the work of St. Thomas: the order and the mystery.

Anticipating a probable objection by critics, I myself wish to say quite frankly that the choice of the texts has been determined entirely by the personal feelings of the chooser; so a personal remark may also be allowed here. During this work I had in mind especially my own circle of friends, and I included only such texts as I should like to bring to their notice. This I did in order that the real character of St. Thomas might be made visible to them in this way. Yet after all, the *objective* point of view may balance the *subjective* to a certain extent.

This Thomist Breviary has, I suppose, scarcely been harmed by the fact that the work of selection and translation has been done during my years of service in the army, and had to progress in a not very academic atmosphere. In such changing conditions of life, what has already become familiar is encountered afresh, as if for the first time, and with previously unknown potentialities of understanding. In this way not a few tractates, which I thought I knew very well, at this second meeting have entirely surprised me. It is now my hope that the character of Thomas Aquinas as revealed in this Breviary, may dawn on the reader also, whether already acquainted with it or not, with that morning power of radiation which is usual at a first meeting.

JOSEF PIEPER

The least insight that one can obtain into sublime things is more desirable than the most certain knowledge of lower things (I, 1, 5 ad 1).

I

The order of the parts of the universe to each other exists in virtue of the order of the whole universe to God. (1)

(2) Everything eternal is necessary.

(3) Just as God himself is One, so he also produces unity; not only because each being is one in itself, but also because all things in a certain sense are one perfect unity.

(4) The more unity a thing has, the more perfect is its goodness and power.

(5) The higher a nature is, the more closely related to it is what emanates from it.

(6) Everything imperfect strives after perfection.

(7) The source of every imperfect thing lies necessarily in one perfect being.

(8) The beginning of everything is directed towards its perfection. This is clear in those things

which are done by nature, as well as in those things which are made by art. Thus every beginning of perfection is ordered to the complete perfection, which is realized in the last end.

(9) The higher the rank a thing holds in the universe, the more it ought to participate in that order in which the goodness of the universe consists.

(10) The more perfect a thing is in power and the greater degree of goodness it possesses, the more universal is its striving after goodness and the more it seeks out and accomplishes good in that which is distant from it.

(11) The sign of perfection in lower beings is that they are able to produce things like themselves.

(12) What comes from God is well ordered. Now the order of things consists in this, that they are led to God each one by the others.

(13) The complete perfection of the universe demands that there should be created natures which return to God, not only according to the likeness of their being, but also through their actions. This can only be through the acts of the reason and the will, because God himself

has no other way of acting towards himself. Hence, for the final perfection of the universe, it was necessary that there should be intellectual beings.

(14) Although a thing which adheres firmly to God is better, yet a thing which can either adhere to God or not is also good. Hence that world in which both these kinds of beings are found is better than one in which there is only one kind.

(15) Although a being subject to decay would be of higher degree if it were incorruptible, yet a world composed of both permanent and transitory beings is better than one in which there are only incorruptible beings.

(16) Although spiritual substance is better than corporeal substance, nevertheless a world in which there were only spiritual beings would not be better but rather less perfect.

(17) All movement is derived from something unmoved.

(18) Everything changeable is reduced to a first unmoved being; hence each particular knowledge is also derived from some completely certain knowledge, which is not subject to error.

3

(19) The order of divine providence demands that there should be coincidence and chance in things.

(20) The perfection of the whole of corporeal nature depends in a certain sense on the perfection of man.

(21) The lowest member of a higher class of beings is always found in contact with the highest member of a lower class. Thus the lowest type of animal life scarcely exceeds the life of plants; for example, oysters which have no movement have only the sense of touch and stick to the earth just like plants. Hence the blessed Denis says, *The Divine Wisdom joins the last of the higher kind with the first of the lower kind.* In the genus of corporeal things we can therefore take something supreme, namely the human body, which is united in harmonious equilibrium. It touches the lowest member of a higher class, namely the human soul which, from its mode of understanding, can be perceived to hold the lowest position in the class of intellectual beings. Hence it comes to pass that the intellectual soul is said to be like the horizon or boundary line between corporeal and incorporeal substance, since it is itself an incorporeal substance and yet is the form of the body.

(22) Intellect is the first author and mover of the universe. . . . Hence the last end of the universe must necessarily be the good of the intellect. This, however, is truth. Hence truth must be the last end of the whole universe.

II

> The creature is vanity in so far as it comes from nothingness, but not in so far as it is an image of God. (23)

(24) Even though created beings pass away, they will never sink back into nothingness.

(25) The creature is darkness in so far as it comes out of nothing. But inasmuch as it has its origin from God, it participates in his image and this leads to likeness to him.

(26) God cannot be the cause of a tendency to not-being. Rather the creature has this of itself, in so far as it has developed out of nothing.

(27) The further a being is distant from that which is Being of itself, namely God, the nearer it is to nothingness. But the nearer a being stands to God, the further away it is from nothingness.

(28) The movement proper to the nature of a creature is not a tendency towards nothingness: this movement has a fixed direction towards

good and the tendency towards nothingness is only a defect in it.

(29) Since free will comes from nothingness, it is its peculiar property not to be naturally confirmed in good.

(30) The property of being pliant to evil belongs to the will in virtue of its origin from nothingness and not because it comes from God.

(31) The intellectual creature cannot naturally be relieved of the possibilities of sinning; since it has arisen out of nothingness, it can be capable of defect.

(32) It is clearly not a convincing argument to say that what is derived from nothing tends of itself to nothingness and thus the potency to not-being resides in all created things. For beings created by God can only be said to tend towards nothing in the same way as they have also taken their origin from nothing. This, however, happens only through the power of the agent. Hence the potency to not-being does not dwell in creatures, but God has the power either to give them being or to allow the inflow of being into them to dry up.

(33) Even that which is stable in things would sink

back into nothingness, since it arises from nothing, were it not held up by the hand of the governor of all things.

(34) The potency to not-being of spiritual creatures dwells more in God, who can withdraw the influx of his power, than in the nature of those creatures themselves.

(35) If God were to reduce a being to nothingness, he would not do it by an action, but because he would cease to act.

III

There can be good without evil; but there cannot be evil without good. (36)

(37) Every creature participates in goodness in the same degree as it participates in being.

(38) Everything that is, and in whatever way it is, is good in so far as it exists.

(39) Being itself is like goodness. *Good* and *Being* are convertible ideas.

(40) *Good* and *true* and *being* are one and the same thing in reality, but in the mind they are distinguished from each other.

(41) Good and the inclination to good follow from the very nature of a being; hence, so long as the nature remains, the inclination to good cannot be removed, not even from the damned.

(42) No essence is in itself evil. Evil has no essence.

(43) Evil consists entirely in not-being.

(44) Nothing can be called evil in so far as it has being, but only in so far as it is deprived of part of its being.

(45) Evil actions are good and come from God in so far as it is a question of the being they possess.

(46) All that belongs to being and action in a sinful act comes from God as first cause. But the deformity in it goes back to free will as its cause, just as the progress made by one who limps is reduced to the power of movement as its first cause, while all the obliquity in such a gait arises from the crookedness of his limbs.

(47) There is nothing unseemly in the thought that God acts with adulterers in their natural action, for the nature of adulterers is not evil, only their will. What is worked by the power of their seed springs not from their will but from their nature. Hence it is not unfitting that God should co-operate in that action and give it its final perfection.

(48) In the demons one is aware of both their nature, which is from God, and the deformity of their sin, which is not from God. Thus it is not absolutely true to say that God is in the demons: we must add—only in so far as they are real beings. But it is absolutely true to say that God

is in things, if we mean things whose nature is not deformed.

(49) Since the demons are intellectual substances, they can in no way have a natural urge to any evil whatsoever. Hence they cannot naturally be evil.

(50) Evil itself is not a positive thing, but that in which evil adheres is something positive, in so far as evil takes away only a part of the good. In the same way, blindness is not anything positive, but he who happens to be blind is something positive.

(51) Just as perfection is comprehended under the word *good*, so the word *evil* means nothing but the loss of perfection.

(52) Evil arises through some particular thing being lacking, but good arises only from a whole and integral cause.

(53) A single and solitary defect is sufficient to make something bad. But for a thing to be absolutely good a single, particular goodness is not sufficient; for this the entire fulness of goodness is demanded.

(54) Every being is perfect in so far as it has real

existence but imperfect in so far as it is only potential, and thus deprived of real existence.

(55) Good is what all things desire, as was first said so well by the Philosopher. . . . But all things in their own way desire real, actual being. This is evident from the fact that all things by their very nature fight against corruption. Hence real, actual being makes up the idea of the good.

(56) The good fulfills not only the idea of being perfect but also that of causing perfection.

(57) Although everything is good in so far as it has being, yet being is not itself the essence of a created thing. Hence it does not follow that a creature is good in virtue of its own essence.

(58) Everything naturally desires unity just as it also desires goodness.

(59) There is no desire which is not directed towards a good.

(60) Nobody can strive after evil for its own sake.

(61) Sin does not occur in the will without some ignorance in the intellect. For we will nothing unless it is good, either real or apparent.

(62) It is impossible that any evil should be striven after precisely as evil, either by the natural appetite, or the sensitive, or the intellectual, which is the will.

(63) We do not strive towards evil by tending towards anything but by turning away from something. Just as a thing is called good by reason of its participation in goodness, so a thing is called evil by reason of its turning away from good.

(64) Evil in things lies outside any purpose: it occurs without the intention of the agent.

(65) Even if that which is aimed at in sin is something evil in reality and opposed to the rational nature, nevertheless it is apprehended as a good and according to nature.

(66) Evil is never loved except under the aspect of good; that is to say, in so far as it is truly a good in some particular respect, but is conceived as absolutely good.

(67) To will evil is neither freedom nor a part of freedom.

(68) Pain at the loss of something good shows the goodness of the nature.

(69) Hatred would never overcome love, except for the sake of a still greater love.

(70) The rational, intellectual nature is related to good and evil in a way which distinguishes it above all other beings. For every other creature is naturally ordered to some particular, partial good. On the other hand, only the intellectual nature apprehends the universal idea of good itself through its intellectual knowledge, and is moved by the desire of the will to the good in its universality. Hence, among rational creatures, evil is divided in a particular way, namely, into fault and punishment.

(71) In the sphere of free-will every evil is either punishment or fault. Fault comes nearer than punishment to the idea of evil.

(72) Punishment is opposed to the good of the one who is punished and deprived of some good. Fault stands in opposition to the good of the order towards God, and thus it is directly opposed to the divine goodness.

(73) Judgment must not be passed on things according to the opinion of the wicked, but according to that of the good, just as in matters of taste, judgment must not be according to the opinion of the sick, but according to that of the healthy.

Hence punishment is not to be regarded as the greater evil, because the wicked are more afraid of it; but fault must rather be held as the greater evil, because the good are more afraid of it.

(74) To the order of the universe there also belongs the order of justice, which demands that punishment should be inflicted on everyone who sins. In this respect, God is the author of the evil which is punishment, but not of the evil which is fault.

(75) It is thus determined in the order of divine justice: that one is subject in punishment to the power of him by whose suggestion one has consented to sin.

(76) Evil must be avoided in every way; hence it is in no way permitted to do evil so that from it some good may arise. But good need not be done in every way; hence some good must sometimes be omitted in order that great evils may be avoided.

(77) Just as good is naturally prior to evil, which signifies a lack of good, so the affections of the soul, whose object is good, are naturally prior to those affections whose object is evil, and which therefore arise from the former. Hence

hatred and sadness have their cause in some love, desire or pleasure.

(78) Good is the cause of evil in so far as it can have a cause at all. For it must be realised that evil cannot have a cause, proper to itself.

(79) Evil is not caused except by good.

(80) Every evil is based on some good. . . . Moral evil is based on the good rooted in human nature; evil which springs from the nature and is the privation of being, is based on matter which is good, like being which only exists potentially.

(81) Everything evil is rooted in some good, and everything false in some truth.

(82) Evil produces no effect except in virtue of some good.

(83) Evil does not fight against good except in virtue of good. For in itself it is powerless and weak, and is the source of no activity.

(84) However much evil is multiplied, it is never able completely to swallow up good.

(85) Stronger than the evil in wickedness is the good in goodness.

(86) Good can be realised in purer form than evil. For there is some good in which no evil is mixed, but there is nothing so very evil that no good is mixed in it.

(87) Though evil always lessens good, yet it is never able completely to destroy it. Just as in this way some good always remains, so there cannot be anything completely and wholly evil.

(88) There can be no supreme evil in the same way as there is a supreme good, which is essentially good.

(89) In the world nothing is found which is wholly and completely evil.

(90) In every sinful action there remains something good.

(91) Nothing is so very evil that it cannot have some appearance of good; and by reason of such goodness it is able to move the desire.

(92) It is impossible for the good of our nature to be destroyed completely by sin.

(93) It is not impossible that an evil should be ordered to good by some good; but it is impossible that anything should be ordered to evil by some good.

(94) If evil were completely excluded from reality, it would mean that much good would also be taken away. Divine providence does not imply the complete removal of evil from reality, but rather the ordering to some good of the evil which arises.

(95) Many good things would disappear if God did not allow some evil to exist.

(96) If God had taken away from the world everything which man has made an occasion of sin, the universe would remain imperfect.

(97) If evil were taken away from some parts of the universe, then much of its perfection would disappear, for its beauty arises from the orderly union of good and evil, while evil springs from the waning away of good. Nevertheless, by the foresight of the governor of the universe, good follows from evil just as the song receives its sweetness from the interval of silence.

IV

Intellectual natures have a greater affinity to the whole than other beings. (98)

(99) In the universe only the intellectual nature is sought on its own account, all others on account of it.

(100) The highest step in the whole process of generation of creatures is the human soul, towards which matter tends as its ultimate form. . . . Man is therefore the end of all generation.

(101) It follows that spiritual things are called *great* according to their fullness of being. For Augustine says that, among those things which have no size, to be greater is the same as to be better.

(102) Intellectual natures have a greater affinity to the whole than other beings; for every intellectual being is in a certain manner all things, in so far as it is able to comprehend all being by the power of its understanding. Every other nature possesses only an imperfect participation in being.

(103) The desire of man is to know something whole and perfect.

(104) The soul is given to man in the place of all the forms, so that in a certain sense man might be all things.

(105) The natural perfection of each single being which is in the state of potentiality consists in the fact that it can be made actual. But the intellect is in the state of potentiality with regard to things which can be known. Before it is made actual it is imperfect; but it is made perfect when it is carried over into the act, so that it arrives at the knowledge of things. Hence some philosophers, directing their attention to the natural perfection of man, have said that the final happiness of man consists in this— that in his soul is reflected the order of the whole universe. . . . Man's beatitude consists in the knowledge of God but not in the knowledge of created things. Hence one is not more blessed because of the knowledge of creatures, but only because of the knowledge of God. Nevertheless, this very knowledge of created things belongs to the natural perfection of the soul.

(106) It is said that the soul is in a certain sense all things, because it is created to know all things. In this way it is possible for the perfection of

the whole universe to have its existence in one single being. Hence, according to philosophers, the ultimate perfection to which the soul can attain is that in it is reflected the whole order of the universe and its causes. This also, they say, is the last end of man, which in our opinion will be attained in the vision of God. *What is there that they will not see, who will see him who sees all things?* (Gregory the Great).

(107) Only the intellectual creature is able to comprehend the direction by which it is directed to its own acts.

(108) It is clear that man is not only a soul but a compound of soul and body. But Plato was able to assert that man is a soul which makes use of the body, because he attributed sense perception to the soul as proper to it.

(109) In so far as the soul is the form of the body, it has not got an existence apart from the existence of the body; it is rather united to the body through this existence.

(110) Union with the body belongs to the essence of the soul.

(111) Since the soul is only a part of human nature,

it does not possess its natural perfection except in union with the body.

(112) Hence our body is transitory because it is not itself perfectly subject to the soul; for were it completely subject to the soul, immortality would overflow to it from the immortality of the soul.

(113) It is clear that the better a body is prepared, the better will be the soul allotted to it. . . . Since among men there are some who possess a better-disposed body, to them also will be allotted a soul endowed with a greater power of understanding.

(114) Since the body with which the intellectual soul is united must be prepared in the best way, it is necessary for the sensitive nature to possess the finest possible organ of the sense of touch. Hence it is said that among all sensitive beings we have the most reliable sense of touch, and also that it is on account of the delicacy of this sense that one man is more fitted than another for the work of the intellect (Aristotle).

(115) All the other senses are based on the sense of touch. . . . Among all beings which have sense perception, man has the most delicate sense of touch. . . . And among men, those who possess

the more refined sense of touch have the best intelligence.

(116) Since man possesses intellect and sense perception and bodily strength, so, according to the plan of divine providence, these are all harmonized in him, in the likeness of that order which is found in the universe.

(117) The human soul possesses such an abundance of various powers because it dwells on the borders of spiritual and material being; in it therefore the powers of both kinds of being meet together.

(118) Natural things learn nothing and forget nothing. . . . We do not forget nor do we learn natural things.

(119) In man there is not only memory but also retrospection.

(120) A devil knows the nature of human thought better than man does.

(121) In us there is not only the pleasure which we share with the beasts, but also the pleasure which we share with the angels.

V

Our intellect in understanding is extended to infinity. (122)

(123) Desire of the knowledge of truth is peculiar to human nature.

(124) In its active nature the intellect is therefore naturally capable of knowing everything that exists.

(125) Wonder is the desire for knowledge.

(126) Our intellect in knowing anything is extended to infinity. This ordering of the intellect to infinity would be vain and senseless if there were no infinite object of knowledge.

(127) An ever-so-imperfect knowledge of most sublime things still implies high perfection for the soul. Hence, although the human reason is unable perfectly to comprehend what lies beyond its limits, nevertheless it acquires much perfection for itself if it, at least in some way. perceives it by faith.

(128) The greatest kindness one can render to any man consists in leading him from error to truth.

(129) The distinction between intelligent beings and those which have no knowledge lies in the fact that the latter have nothing but their own form, while intelligent beings have the forms of other things also, since the image of the thing known is in the knower. Hence it is clear that the nature of non-intelligent beings is narrower and more restricted, while that of intelligent beings has greater breadth and power of comprehension. Hence the Philosopher says that the soul is in a certain manner all things.

(130) The most perfect types of beings, such as intellectual beings, make the most complete return to their own essences. In knowing something outside themselves, they step outside themselves in a certain sense; in so far as they know that they know, they already begin to return to themselves, for the act of knowledge is midway between the knower and the thing known. But that return is completely achieved when they know their own essences. Hence every being which knows its own essence is said to make the most perfect return to its essence.

(131) To return to its own essence is nothing other than having independent being resting in itself.

(132) The proper object of the human intellect when united with the body is natures actually existing in corporeal matter.

(133) Our natural knowledge can extend as far as it can be led by the hand through material things.

(134) Since the senses are the first source of our knowledge, it follows that all things upon which we pass judgment are necessarily related to the senses in some way.

(135) Although the soul is more like God than other creatures are, yet it cannot arrive at knowledge of its own nature, so as to distinguish it from other natures, except by way of creatures which can be known by the senses, and from which our knowledge takes its origin.

(136) Although by Revelation we are elevated to the knowledge of things which would otherwise remain unknown to us, yet we are never raised so far as to know them in any way other than through things which can be known by the senses.

(137) The senses are not deceived concerning their proper object.

(138) Truth is in both the reason and the sense-faculties, but not in the same way. It is in the reason as the result of the act of knowledge, and at the same time as known by the reason. . . .

It is known by the reason because the reason is reflected on its own act, knowing not only its act but also its relation to reality. . . . In the sense-faculties, however, truth is only the result of their act. . . . But it is not in the sense-faculties as known by the senses. Though the sense-faculties make true judgments on things, yet they do not know the truth by which they make true judgments. For though the senses know that they perceive things, yet they do not know their own nature, and consequently the nature of their act, its relation to reality and its truth remain unknown by the senses.

(139) No sense organ is aware of itself or of its operation. The eye neither sees itself, nor does it see that it sees. But the intellect is aware of itself and of its act of knowing.

(140) To judge one's own judgment: this can only be done by the reason, which reflects on its own act and knows the relation between that upon which it judges and that by which it judges. Hence the root of all freedom lies in the reason.

(141) The object of the natural appetite is in every case *this thing* in so far as it is *this thing*. The object of the sensitive appetite is always *this thing* in so far as it is agreeable and brings pleasure; for example, water not in so far as it

is water, but precisely as pleasing to the taste. But the proper object of the will is the good itself, taken as such. In the same way sense perception is distinguished from intellectual knowledge: the apprehension of *this coloured thing* is proper to the senses, but the intellect knows the very nature of colour itself.

(142) The truth of the human intellect receives its direction and measurement from the essences of things. For the truth or falsity of an opinion depends on whether a thing is or is not.

(142a) The most perfect kind of order is found in things; from them is derived the order of our knowledge.

(143) The human intellect is measured by things so that man's thought is not true on its own account but is called true in virtue of its conformity with things. . . . The divine intellect, on the other hand, is the measure of things, since things are true to the extent in which they represent the divine intellect.

(144) Created things are midway between God's knowledge and our knowledge, for we receive our knowledge from things which are caused by God's knowledge. Hence just as things which can be known are prior to our knowledge and

are its measure, so is God's knowledge the measure of created things and prior to them.

(145) The word has naturally more conformity with the reality it expresses than with the person who speaks, even though it dwells in the speaker as in its subject.

(146) Nobody perceives himself to know except from the fact that he knows some object, because knowledge of some object is prior to knowledge of oneself as knowing. Hence the soul expressly attains to the perception of itself only through that which it knows or perceives. . . . Our mind is unable to know itself in such a way that it immediately apprehends itself, but it arrives at knowledge of itself by the fact that it perceives other things.

(147) It is necessary to say that the human soul knows all things in the eternal ideas as all our knowledge arises from participation in them. The intellectual light dwelling in us is nothing else than a kind of participated image of the uncreated light in which the eternal ideas are contained.

(148) Just as in that part of the soul adapted to active operation, the first intuitive awareness of principles never errs, so insight into the first prin-

ciples of knowledge never errs in that part of the soul which is disposed to speculative reasoning.

(149) A twofold relationship is found between the soul and reality. One is when the real thing is itself in the soul in the manner of the soul and not in its own mode: the other is when the soul is related to the real thing existing in its own mode of being. Thus a thing is the object of the soul in a double way. One way is in so far as the thing is disposed or adapted to be in the soul, not according to its own mode of being, but in the manner of the soul; that is to say, in a spiritual way. This is the idea of intelligibility in so far as it is knowable. In the other way, a real thing is the object of the soul inasmuch as the soul is inclined to it and ordered to it according to the mode of real being existing in itself. This is the idea of desirability in so far as it is desirable.

(150) Knowledge takes place in the degree in which the thing known is in the knower, but love takes place inasmuch as the lover is united with the real object of his love. Higher things exist in a nobler way in themselves than in lower things but, on the other hand, lower things exist in a nobler way in higher things than in themselves. Hence knowledge of lower things is more valuable than love of them, but love of higher

things, and above all love of God, is more valuable than knowledge.

(151) Love of God is better than knowledge of him; on the other hand, knowledge of corporeal things is better than love of them. Nevertheless, considered in itself, the intellect is nobler than the will.

(152) Knowledge is perfected by the thing known becoming one with the knower in its image. Love, however, causes the very thing itself which is loved to become one with the lover in a certain sense. Hence love has more unitive power than knowledge.

(153) Union belongs to love in so far as the loving desire is related in affection to the thing loved as to itself or something belonging to itself.

(154) Intellectual activity is made perfect in that intelligible things are in the intellect according to its own proper mode of being. Hence the intellect is not injured but is made perfect by things. The action of the will, on the other hand, consists in movement towards the thing itself, so that in love the soul is fused together with the thing loved. Hence the soul receives some blemish when it clings to things in an inordinate way.

(155) There is the following distinction between the intellect and the will. Knowledge is caused by the fact that the thing known is in a certain way in the knower. The will, however, does not act in the same way, but contrariwise, according as the will is related to the actual thing desired, in so far as the one who wills seeks something in which he finds satisfaction. For this reason good and evil, which are concerned with the will, are in things; but truth and error, which are concerned with the intellect, are in the mind which knows.

(156) Love is said to transform the lover into the loved because by love the lover is moved towards the thing loved. But knowledge creates likeness in so far as an image of the thing known arises in the knower.

(157) Truth and goodness include one another. The truth is something good; otherwise it would not be worth desiring; and the good is true; otherwise it would not be intelligible.

(158) Since goodness and truth are convertible in reality, it follows that the good is known by the mind as true just as truth is desired by the will as good.

(159) Truth is the good of the intellect; for this

reason every intellect is called good because it knows truth.

(160) The will would never desire knowledge unless the intellect first of all comprehended knowledge itself as something good.

(161) The good, considered as true, is related to the reason before it is related to the will as something worth desiring.

(162) The intellect is in itself prior to the will, because the object of the will is a good which is known, yet the will is prior in action and in movement.

(163) Every act of the will arises from an act of the intellect. Nevertheless, one particular act of the will is prior to a particular act of the intellect, for the will tends towards the final act of the intellect, which is beatitude.

(164) The will is not a supreme rule but is a rule receiving its direction from elsewhere, because it is directed by the reason and intellect, not only in us but also in God. In us intellect and will are really distinct, and hence the will and the rectitude of the will are also not the same, but in God intellect and will are the same in

reality, and hence the rectitude of his will is also identical with his will itself.

(165) In a certain sense the will always obeys itself; namely, so that man in some way always wills that which he wishes to will. In one sense, however, it does not always obey itself; namely, when one wills imperfectly and ineffectively what he wished to will perfectly and effectively.

(166) The perfection of goodness is more widespread than that of truth. . . . All beings strive after the good, but not all know the truth.

(167) It would seem that God cannot be loved directly in this life, for *one cannot love what one does not know*, as Augustine says. But we do not know God directly in this life: *we see him through a glass darkly* (1 Cor. 13.12). Hence we do not love him directly.—To this we must reply: Although one cannot love what one does not know, yet the order of knowledge need not necessarily be the same as that of love. Love is the term or end of knowledge; hence it can begin at once where knowledge ceases, namely, in the thing itself which is known through another thing.

(168) The intellect knows not only for itself, but also for all the powers of the soul. The will wills not

only for itself, but also for all the powers of the soul.

(169) Man wills good by natural necessity.

(170) The proper object of love is the good. . . . The good is the proper cause of love.

(171) Everything that acts, whatever it may be, performs every action from some kind of love.

(172) Just as natural movement and rest spring from the form of a thing, so every affection of the soul has its origin in love.

(173) Love is the first movement of the will and every faculty of desire.

(174) In us love receives its order from virtue.

(175) The first act of the will does not exist in virtue of the command of the reason, but in virtue of a natural instinct or some higher cause.

VI

Morality presupposes nature. (176)

(177) Natural love resides not only in the powers of the vegetative soul but also in all the powers of the soul and in every part of the body, and universally in all things.

(178) The first source to which every act of the will is reduced is that which is willed naturally by man.

(179) Just as natural knowledge is always true, so is natural love always good, since it is nothing other than a natural urge implanted by the author of nature. Hence, to say that a natural inclination is wrong is to offer an insult to the creator of nature.

(180) In the same way as the will is founded on nature, everything that is desired has its origin and foundation in something which is naturally desired.

(181) The right order of things is in harmony with the order of nature, for natural things are ordered to their end without any error.

(182) Reason imitates nature.

(183) The principles of reason are those which are conformed to nature.

(184) It is certain that what the reason is naturally endowed with is true in the highest degree; so much so that it is not even possible to think it can be false.

(185) Since the will is naturally good, its natural act is always good. As man wills his own happiness naturally, the natural act of the will is understood to be life and beatitude. If we are referring to moral good, then the will considered in itself is neither good nor bad, but is in potency to good and evil.

(186) In the sphere of intellectual knowledge and voluntary action, what is natural comes first, and from it all else is derived. From the knowledge of naturally known first principles is derived the knowledge of that which follows from them, and from the fact that one wills the end naturally perceived is derived the choice of the means leading to the end.

(187) Action conformable to art and reason must be uniform with that which is according to nature and instituted by the divine reason.

(188) A natural desire cannot possibly be vain and senseless.

(189) Nature is presupposed by all the virtues, those bestowed gratuitously by God as well as those which are acquired.

(190) To become like nature by consenting to the reason is the property of those virtues dwelling in the appetite.

(191) Just as the order of right reason takes its origin from man, so the order of nature is from God himself.

(192) Natural inclinations dwell in things by the action of God, who moves all things. Hence it is impossible that the natural tendency of any kind of being should be directed to something which is evil in itself. But the natural urge to carnal intercourse resides in all perfect animals. It is therefore impossible that carnal intercourse should be evil in itself.

(193) Even in the state of innocence there would have been generation of offspring for the multiplication of the human race; otherwise man's sin would have been necessary in order that so great a good should arise from it.

(194) Perhaps you may say: If the Word has assumed a living body, why then did the Evangelist make no mention of the spiritual soul but only of the flesh, when he says, *The Word was made flesh?* To this I answer: the Evangelist did this firstly in order to manifest the reality of the Incarnation against the Manichees, who said the Word did not take on real flesh . . . since it is not fitting that the word of the good God should take on flesh, which they themselves called a creature of the devil.

(195) Since that which is according to nature is ordered by the divine reason, which ought to be imitated by human reason, hence sin and evil is whatever is done by human judgment contrary to the order which is commonly found in natural things.

(196) Everything that opposes a natural inclination is sinful because it is contrary to the law of nature.

(197) Sin is opposed to the natural inclination.

(198) Since sin is contrary to nature . . . to seek the satisfaction of a natural desire is not sinful if nothing inordinate is added to it.

(199) The virtues perfect us so that we follow our natural inclinations in a fitting manner.

(200) The natural inclination is the beginning of virtue.

(201) Although the virtues in their perfect state do not have their origin in nature, yet they cause an inclination to that which is according to nature, that is to say, that which is according to the order of reason.

(202) The submission of the lower powers of the soul to reason comes from nature, but they are not actually and continually subject by their nature.

(203) The natural inclination to the good of virtue is indeed a beginning of virtue, but it is not perfect virtue. The more perfect such an inclination, the more dangerous can it be, if it is not united to right reason . . . just as when a racing horse is blind, the more impetuously it dashes forward, the more violently does it collide with some object and the more grievously is it injured.

(204) There can be a natural inclination to the acts of a single virtue but not to the acts of all the virtues, because the natural readiness by which a man is inclined to one virtue at the same time causes an inclination to the contrary of another virtue. He who happens to have a natural predisposition to fortitude, which is manifested in

the prosecution of a difficult end, is less disposed to meekness, which consists in mastering the passions of the irascible powers.

(205) Every sin is based on a natural desire. Since man naturally desires likeness to God, in so far as all naturally desired goodness is an image of the divine goodness, hence Augustine says, when speaking to God: *The soul commits adultery— in sinning—when it turns aside from Thee and seeks outside Thee those things which it can find pure and clear only when it returns to Thee.*

VII

Reason is man's nature. Hence whatever is contrary to reason is contrary to human nature. (206)

(207) What is ordered according to reason is according to human nature.

(208) The good of man, precisely as man, consists in this: that the reason should be perfect in the knowledge of truth, and that the subordinate affections should be regulated in accordance with the rule of reason. For man's human nature belongs to him from the fact that he has the power of reason.

(209) The rule of the human will is twofold. One is immediate and homogeneous, namely, the human reason. The other is the supreme rule, namely, the eternal law, which is, so to speak, God's reason.

(210) The human will can only be protected from sin when the reason is preserved from ignorance and error.

(211) Moral virtue perfects the appetitive faculty of man by directing it towards the good of the reason.

(212) Human nature in the strict sense consists in being according to the reason. Hence a man is said to contain himself when he acts in accordance with reason.

(213) The more necessary something is, the more it needs the preservation of the order of reason in it.

(214) Moral virtue is nothing other than a participation of the appetite in right reason.

(215) The perfection of virtue is achieved not by nature but by the reason.

(216) The reason which knows evil is not opposed to good but rather shares in the idea of good.

(217) The root cause of human good is the reason.

(218) Human good is the end of the moral virtues; but the good of the human soul is to be in accordance with reason.

(219) The reason is the primary source of all human activity. Those sources of human action which

are also found elsewhere, in some way obey the reason.

(220) Every movement of the appetite conformed to true knowledge is good in itself; but every movement conformed to false knowledge is in itself bad and sinful.

(221) The spiritual beauty of the soul consists in the fact that the conduct and action of man is in accordance with and fitted to the spiritual clearness of the reason.

(222) Considered in itself the will which departs from the reason is always bad, no matter whether it is right or wrong.

(223) Although a man is not superior to himself, yet the one, by whose command he has knowledge, is superior to him; thus man is bound by his own conscience.

(224) When the reason proposes something to us as God's command, then, even if it is in error, to despise the command of the reason is the same as despising God's command.

(225) Conscience is said to be the law of our minds because it is the verdict of the reason, deduced from the law of nature.

(226) Man himself does not create the law; but through his knowledge, by which he perceives the law created by someone else, he is bound to obey the law.

(227) To compare the obligation of conscience with the obligation due to the command of a superior is the same as comparing the obligation of a divine command with the obligation of a superior's command. Since a divine command binds even against the order of a superior and in a higher way, the obligation of conscience is thus higher than the obligation of a superior's command, and the conscience will bind even if it conflicts with the command of a superior.

VIII

The desire of the last end is not among those things over which we have mastery. (228)

(229) Wherever there is intellectual knowledge, there is also free will.

(230) He who acts against his will has no freedom of action, but he can truly have free will.

(231) The nature of free will is not the ability to choose evil; but the choice of evil is a consequence of free will, in so far as the latter resides in a created nature which is capable of defect.

(232) We are masters of our actions inasmuch as we are able to choose this or that. Choice, however, is not concerned with the end, but only with the means leading to the end. Hence desire of the last end is not among those things over which we have mastery.

(233) The will necessarily desires its last end so that it is unable not to desire it; but it does not necessarily desire any of the means leading to the end.

(234) Anything towards which we strive naturally is not subject to free will.

(235) Every appetitive nature must necessarily desire peace, since it always strives to arrive peacefully and without hindrance at that towards which its desire goes out.

(236) Whoever strives towards good, by this very fact also desires beauty. . . . It is the same desire that is directed towards goodness, beauty and peace.

(237) The end is last in execution but first in the intention of the reason.

(238) Man necessarily desires everything on account of the last end.

(239) Man is not called simply good when he is good in some part only, but when he is good in his entirety; but the latter comes about through the goodness of the will.

(240) A good man is not one who has a good intellect but one who has a good will.

(241) A good will makes a man absolutely good.

(242) The man who has a good will is called simply a good man.

(243) Rightness of intention alone does not make the will completely good.

(244) From the fact that one wills the end, the reason determines on the means leading to the end.

(245) Whenever a colour is seen, light is perceived at the same time; but one can see light without perceiving colour.* In the same way, whenever the means to an end are willed, the end is willed at the same time; but the converse does not hold good.

---

*The theory of light which St. Thomas inherited from Aristotle is now known to be quite erroneous. What he means by the words, "one can see light without perceiving colour," is that though the "diaphanous" —i.e., air, ether, or atmosphere—is not visible in itself as colours are, yet it may be said to be seen in the same sense as we say we see darkness.

IX

The happiness of the active life lies in the action of prudence by which man rules himself and others. (246)

(247) Three things are necessary for the salvation of man: to know what he ought to believe, to know what he ought to desire, and to know what he ought to do.

(248) The will is directed to the end, but choice to that which leads to the end.

(249) A man does not take counsel with himself over the end, but only over the means leading to the end.

(250) To order is the task of the wise man.

(251) The name of wise man simply in itself is reserved only for him whose consideration is directed to the end of the universe, which is also the source of all things.

(252) Even though knowledge of universals is first

in certainty, yet it does not have first place in the sphere of operation; that belongs rather to knowledge of particulars, since action is concerned with particular things.

(253) It is not the task of prudence to concern itself with the most sublime things, which are considered by wisdom. Prudence rules the things which are ordered to wisdom, namely the means by which men ought to arrive at wisdom. In this way prudence is the servant of wisdom.

(254) Prudence considers the ways by which we arrive at beatitude: but wisdom considers the very object of beatitude.

(255) Man already possesses some share in true beatitude according to the measure in which he studies wisdom.

(256) By wisdom itself one is led to the everlasting kingdom (Wisd. 6.21).

(257) Moral virtue presupposes knowledge.

(258) Since practical knowledge belongs to prudence, it is more natural to man than pure speculative knowledge.

(259) Human virtue is perfection in a human way.

Man is not able to comprehend the truth of things with certainty in a simple intuition, especially those things which are related to action and contingent.

(260) The happiness of the contemplative life lies in nothing else but the perfect consideration of the highest truth; but the happiness of the active life lies in the act of prudence, through which man rules himself and others.

(261) The more contemplation excels the active life, the more service seems to be done for God by one who has to put up with a loss of his beloved contemplation in order to serve the salvation of his neighbour for God's sake.

(262) A precious pearl is more valuable than bread; but in the case of hunger bread would be preferred to it.

(263) He who is dying of hunger must be fed rather than taught, since for one in need *it is better to inherit wealth than to be a philosopher* (Aristotle), although the latter in itself is certainly of higher value.

(264) To be called from the contemplative to the active life is not a loss but a gain.

(265) All the virtues of the appetitive part of man, which are called the moral virtues, in so far as they are virtues are caused by prudence.

(266) When things are lower than the one who knows them, then to know them is superior to willing what is directed towards them, because then things are in a higher way in the intellect than in themselves—since everything that is in something else is in it in the manner of that thing in which it is. But when things are higher than the one who knows them, then the will ascends higher than the mind is able to reach. Thus it comes about that in the sphere of moral action, which is lower than man himself, an intellectual virtue gives their form to the moral virtues—as prudence to the other moral virtues. In the sphere of the theological virtues, however, which are directed towards God, charity, which is a virtue of the will, gives its form to faith, which is an intellectual virtue.

(267) To prudence belongs the execution of all precepts about the acts of justice contained in the law.

(268) The act of the (sensitive) desire is imperfect unless reason is perfected by prudence, no matter what disposition to good may dwell in the appetitive faculty. Without prudence, there-

fore, there cannot be discipline, or moderation, or any moral virtue.

(269) Prudence is wisdom in human affairs, but not wisdom absolutely in itself. Prudence is directed to human good, but man is not the highest good in the sphere of existing beings.

(270) All moral virtue must be prudent.

(271) All sins are opposed to prudence, just as all virtues are ruled by prudence.

(272) Prudence helps all the other virtues and acts in them all.

(273) In general, man can receive counsel from another regarding that which is to be done; but, in the very act itself, the preservation of his judgment in undisturbed rectitude against the influence of the passions arises only from the unerring rule of prudence, without which there can be no virtue.

(274) In matters of prudence nobody is self-sufficient in all things.

(275) Those who need to be guided by the advice of another, if they are in a state of grace, at least know how to advise themselves by the fact that

they seek the advice of someone else and are able to distinguish good and bad counsel.

(276) In human activity a special kind of prudence is found wherever there is a special kind of domination and ordering.

(277) A man cannot be sufficiently prudent in the domain of a single virtue unless he is prudent in all things.

(278) When man acts against any virtue he acts against prudence, without which there cannot be any moral virtue.

(279) Prudence is frustrated chiefly by intemperance. . . . Hence the vices opposed to prudence arise mostly from impurity.

X

Moral virtue does not exclude the passions. (280)

(281) The passions are in themselves neither good nor bad, since in man good and evil are determined according to the reason. Hence the passions, considered in themselves, can be good as well as evil, according as they can correspond with the reason or be contrary to it.

(282) What is good is determined for every being according to the condition of its nature. Hence good human action is accompanied by passion and the service of the body.

(283) Since human nature is made up of body and soul, of an intellectual and a sensitive part, human good demands that man should surrender himself in his totality to virtue; that is to say, both in his intellectual and sensitive part, and with his body. Hence, for human virtue it is necessary that the desire for just vengeance should reside not only in the rational part of the soul but also in the sensitive part and in the body, and that the body should be moved to serve virtue.

(284) Hence it is true that *to act from passion* lessens both praise and blame, but *to act with passion* can increase both.

(285) It is not contrary to the idea of virtue that the deliberation of the reason should be suspended in the carrying out of that which has already been considered by the reason.

(286) He who is angry or afraid is not praised or blamed, but only he who, while in this state, behaves either properly or not.

(287) There are four basic passions of the soul— Sadness, Joy, Hope and Fear.

(288) Like nature, passion also drives itself violently to one determined thing.

(289) Of all the passions, sadness causes the most injury to the soul.

(290) Every virtue by which a passion is ordered also gives order to the body.

(291) Anger, it is true, in some way upsets the reason, even if it follows a rational judgment, but it helps the promptitude of action.

(292) Anger, like all other movements of the sensitive

appetite, is useful from the fact that when angry a man does more readily what reason commands.* Otherwise the sensitive appetite in man would be in vain, whereas it remains true that nature makes nothing in vain.

(293) Since hatred wills evil to another precisely as evil, it is not satisfied with any degree of evil, since what is desired for its own sake is desired without any limit, as the Philosopher says. . . . Anger, however, wills evil only under the aspect of just vengeance; hence when the evil inflicted exceeds the measure of justice in the opinion of the one who is angry, then he becomes merciful.

(294) Despair, like hope, presupposes desire. Neither hope nor despair is directed towards anything which does not move our desire.

(295) Fear is never without hope in a happy result, which cannot exist in any way in the damned, in whom there can therefore be no fear.

(296) All fear arises from the love of something.

(297) Fear makes men more deliberative than hope.

* Though anger coming after a rational judgment upsets the reason, nevertheless it is useful because it gives greater promptitude in carrying out the commands of the reason. Coming before a judgment, however, anger is bad, as it makes a true judgment almost impossible.

XI

Through virtue man is ordered to the utmost limit of his capacity. (298)

(299) Sin consists in the loss of order in the soul, just as sickness consists in disorder of the body.

(300) Inordinate love of self is the cause of all sin.

(301) All sin arises from some ignorance.

(302) Inordinate fear is included in every sin; the miser fears the loss of money, the intemperate man the loss of pleasure.

(303) Spiritual sins contain a greater malice than those of the flesh.

(304) He who sins turns aside from that in which the idea of the last end is truly found; but, as a matter of fact, he does not cease to intend the last end, which, however, he seeks wrongly in other things.

(305) The good for everything is what is fitting to it according to its form; evil is that which does not correspond to the order of its form.

(306) Sin is nothing other than falling away from the good which is fitting to one's nature.

(307) Virtue is called the limit of potentiality . . . because it causes an inclination to the highest act which a faculty can perform.

(308) The nature of virtue demands that it should look up to the last end.

XII

Pleasure perfects opera-
tion just as beauty per-
fects youth. (309)

(310) All things desire pleasure in the same way as
they desire goodness; but they strive towards
pleasure on account of good and not *e converso*.
It does not thereby follow that pleasure is the
greatest good or that it is good in itself; but
every pleasure does spring from some good, and
some pleasure springs from that which is the
highest good and good in itself.

(311) The fact that children and animals seek pleasure
does not show that they are altogether wicked:
in them the natural impulse acts from God,
who moves them to act according to that impulse.

(312) Pleasure is a kind of perfection of operation,
as the Philosopher has made clear; it perfects
operation just as beauty perfects youth.

(313) The desire strives towards good in the same
way as it strives towards the enjoyment of good,
which is pleasure. Thus as the desire is moved

to action through striving towards good, so also through striving towards pleasure.

(314) The more perfect action causes more perfect pleasure.

(315) In so far as it is loved, everything becomes a source of pleasure.

(316) All pleasure is uniform in that it means the resting in some good, and in this respect it can be a rule and measure of action. He whose will comes to rest in an actual good is himself good, while he whose will comes to rest in evil is himself evil.

(317) Good is aspired to and pleasure is desired for the same reason: this reason is nothing other than the satisfaction of the appetite in good.

(318) The idea of joy is distinguished from that of pleasure. Pleasure arises from a real union with some good thing. Joy, however, does not require this; the mere satisfaction of the will is sufficient for the idea of joy.

(319) Pleasure is not good in the highest degree from the fact that it is pleasure, but because it is perfect rest in a sublime good.

(320) Pleasure which springs from contemplation is opposed by no sadness; nor is sadness joined to it—except in an accidental way.

(321) There is a double goodness common to pleasure and sadness; true judgment on good and evil as well as the due order of the will which accepts good and rejects evil. Thus it is clear that in pain and sadness there is some good the lessening of which can make them less good themselves. But in every pleasure there is not something evil through whose removal the pleasure itself can become better. Hence it is in fact possible that some pleasure can be the highest good of man . . . but sadness cannot be the greatest human evil.

XIII

Grace and virtue imitate the order of nature which is instituted by the divine wisdom. (322)

(323) The act of the intellect is accomplished by the thing known being in the knower; thus the excellence of the intellectual act is determined according to the degree of the intellect. The act of the will, and of every appetitive faculty, is perfected in the inclination of the one who desires to the actual thing desired, as to its end; hence the dignity of the act of the appetite is determined in accordance with the actual thing which is the object of this act. A thing inferior to the soul is in the soul in a nobler way than in itself, for every thing is in another in the manner of that in which it is. A thing higher than the soul, however, is in a nobler way in itself, than in the soul. Hence, with regard to what is inferior to us, knowledge is nobler than love, for which reason the Philosopher places the intellectual virtues higher than the moral virtues. But with regard to what is above us, especially God, love is higher than knowledge. Hence charity excels faith.

(324) The discipline and moderation of the miser, which restrain the desire for intemperance because it may cost money, are not true virtue. ... There can be no true virtue without charity.

(325) Although charity is necessary for salvation, it is not necessary to know that one has charity; rather it is generally more useful not to know.

(326) As it is good to love a friend in so far as he is a friend, so it is bad to love an enemy in so far as he is an enemy; but it is good to love an enemy in so far as he is a creature of God. To love a friend as a friend, and an enemy as an enemy, would be a contradiction; but it is no contradiction to love both friend and enemy in so far as both are creatures of God.

(327) To love an enemy is higher than to love only a friend, since it shows greater love of God. But if we consider both acts in themselves, it is better to love a friend than an enemy, and it is better to love God than a friend. The difficulty involved in loving an enemy does not determine the nature of merit, except inasmuch as it manifests the perfection of love which overcomes this difficulty. Hence, if love were so perfect that it would completely overcome the difficulty, it would be still more meritorious.

(328) In the idea of merit and virtue the good is more valuable than the effort. Hence, not all that is difficult is also meritorious: but it must be difficult in such a way that it is at the same time good in a higher way.

(329) The nature of virtue lies in good more than in difficulty.

(330) The divine law so orders men to each other that each one preserves his order. This means that men have peace with each other, for peace between men, as Augustine says, is nothing other than the harmony of order.

(331) The idea of peace includes the idea of concord and adds something further. Wherever there is peace, there is also concord; but wherever concord rules, there is not always peace, if peace is understood at all in its proper sense. . . . Concord implies one common intention among many people; but peace, in addition to this common purpose, also implies a unity of desire in each individual. Peace is opposed by a twofold dissension; the dissension of men with themselves and the dissension between one another. Only the second kind of dissension opposes concord.

(331a) To be at peace befits love; but to make peace is the work of ordering wisdom.

(332) A father naturally loves his son more than brothers love each other, although the son does not love his father as much as he is loved by him.

(333) The love with which one loves oneself includes the love of wife and child more than the love of father.

(334) The common good is the noblest among human goods; but the divine goodness surpasses human good.

(335) Man cannot possibly be good unless he stands in the right relation to the common good.

(336) The higher virtues are in a closer relation to the common good. But justice and fortitude are more closely related than temperance to the common good.

(337) The good of the whole is higher than the particular good of an individual, if both are understood as springing from the same source. But the good of a single grace is higher than the natural good of the whole universe.

(338) Just as the right use of power in ruling over many people is a good in the highest degree,

so is its misuse in the highest degree evil. Thus power can be turned into good or evil.

(339) God's power is his goodness; hence he can only use his power in a good way. But this is not so in the case of man. Hence it is not sufficient for beatitude that man should become like to God in power, unless he becomes like to him in goodness also.

(340) Every law is ordered to the common salvation of mankind, and it is in virtue of this quality that it possesses the nature and binding force of law. In so far as it fails in this, it has no power of obligation.

(341) Among the virtues only justice includes the idea of duty; hence moral virtue is determinable by law in the degree in which it is related to justice.

(342) The task of the human lawgiver is to rule external actions only. To God alone, who is the divine lawgiver, belongs the ruling of the interior movements of the will.

(343) Human law sets up no precepts except about justice; if it prescribes the acts of other virtues, it does so only in so far as these assume the nature of justice.

(344) Justice without mercy cannot be perfect virtue.

(345) Justice without mercy is cruelty; mercy without justice is the mother of laxity.

(346) Mercy does not cancel out justice; it is rather, in a manner of speaking, the plenitude of justice.

(347) The old and the wise, who think that evil can also happen to themselves, likewise the feeble and the fearful are more merciful. Those, on the contrary, who think themselves to be happy, and so strong that no evil can happen to them, are not so easily merciful. Thus weakness is always a foundation of mercy.*

(348) Among all the moral virtues the activity of right reason appears more particularly in justice. The wrong use of the reason is therefore most apparent in sins against justice.

(349) The good of the reason lies in truth as its proper object and in justice as its proper effect.

(350) The praise of fortitude in a certain sense depends on justice. Hence Ambrose says, *Fortitude without justice is the matter from which evil arises.*

---

* This applies only to man. God's mercy always arises from his love.

(351) To suffer death is not to be praised for its own sake but only because of its order to some good.

(352) Those who do brave deeds for the sake of worldly glory are not truly brave.

(353) It can happen that a man may fear death **less** than he ought.

(354) Fortitude appears to excel among the virtues. Virtue is concerned with things difficult and good. But fortitude is concerned with difficulty; hence it is the greatest of the virtues. To this we must reply: the idea of virtue consists in good rather than difficulty. The greatness of a virtue is therefore to be measured according to the idea of good rather than that of difficulty.

(355) The boldest people are those who are rightly related to divine things.

(356) The acts of fortitude in battle are ordered to victory and peace; for it would be foolish to wage war only for its own sake.

(357) Fortitude has two acts—to attack and to hold one's ground.

(358) The most special act of fortitude, more peculiar to it than attacking, is to sustain, that is to say to stand immovable in the face of danger.

(359) Endurance truly implies a suffering attitude of the body, but it also implies an act of the soul which with all its strength perseveres in good; it follows from this that the soul does not yield to bodily passion already attacking it.

(360) Endurance is more difficult than attacking, and this for three reasons. Firstly, endurance seems to mean that one stands fast against a stronger assailant, while one who attacks goes forward with superior strength; but it is more difficult to fight against a stronger than a weaker opponent. Secondly, endurance perceives danger already present, while for the one who attacks it is still in the future; but it is more difficult to be unmoved by the present than by the future. Thirdly, endurance implies duration in time, while one can attack with a sudden impulse; but it is more difficult to remain unmoved for a long time than to fly at some difficult object with a sudden movement.

(361) A brave man is also patient.

(362) Patience is included in fortitude, for the essential quality of patience is also possessed by the brave, namely not being upset by threatening evil. Fortitude, however, adds something further, namely to attack the threatening evil when necessary.

(363) A man is called patient not because he shuns evil but because he endures a present evil in an honourable fashion; that is to say, he is not made unduly sad by it.

(364) Among the virtues temperance in particular lays claim to a special beauty, and ugliness is most apparent in sins of intemperance.

(365) There is something shameful about all sin, but especially about the sin of intemperance.

(366) Intemperance is most opposed to the purity and beauty of man.

(367) Right reason makes one exercise abstinence *in a fitting way*, namely, with cheerfulness of mind, and *for a fitting end,* namely, for the glory of God and not for the glorification of oneself.

(368) All worldly things can be reduced to three: honour, wealth and happiness.

(369) Abstinence from things which bring pleasure is fitting for those who have undertaken the life of contemplation and the passing on of spiritual good to others in a kind of spiritual generation, but it is not fitting to those whose task it is to do bodily work and serve physical generation.

(370) If a man deliberately abstains from wine to such an extent that he does serious harm to his nature, he will not be free from blame.

(371) Recreation is necessary to lead a human life.

(372) The result of impurity is a harmful duplicity of mind.

(373) The virtue of chastity prepares man best for contemplation.

(374) He who gives way to anger is less worthy of blame than he who yields to desire, for the latter is less deprived of reason.

(375) Sons imitate their fathers more in sins of anger than in sins of desire.

(376) Meekness above all makes men masters of themselves.

(377) Pride extinguishes all the virtues and destroys all the powers of the soul, since its rule extends to them all.

(378) The skilful doctor puts up with his patient being afflicted by a lesser illness in order that he may recover from a serious disorder; in the same way the gravity of sins of pride is shown

by the fact that God allows man to fall into other sins in order to heal him from pride.

(379) Many people take pride even in their humility.

(380) In a certain sense humility is man's readiness to approach spiritual and divine things.

(381) Humility makes man capable of knowing God.

(382) Humility prepares the way for wisdom.

(383) Two things can be considered in man; what is of God and what is of man. . . . In view of this every man must submit what is of man in himself to what is of God in his neighbour. . . . But humility does not demand that a man should submit what is of God in himself to that which seems to be of God in another. . . . In the same way humility does not demand that a man should submit what is of himself to that which is of man in another.

(384) Pusillanimity can also spring from pride.

(385) To act deceitfully is a sign of pusillanimity: but a proud man is open and frank in all things.

(386) The ambitious are easily made jealous. In like

manner the faint-hearted are jealous, as they consider everything to be important, and whatever good falls to someone else, they believe to be an unfair advantage.

XIV

The theologian considers human actions in so far as through them man is ordered to beatitude. (387)

(388) The last end of human life is beatitude.

(389) A man is called a *wayfarer* because he is striving towards beatitude; but he is called a *"comprehensor"* when he has already reached beatitude.

(390) Striving towards beatitude is the same as striving towards the satisfaction of the will.

(391) Happiness is a good proper to human beings. Animals can only be called happy by a misuse of language.

(392) Even though money is merely useful, yet it has a certain resemblance to happiness because it possesses the character of universality, since all things obey money (Eccles. 10.19).*

(393) In perfect beatitude the whole man is made

* For the miser, one who makes money the last end of human life, all things may be said to obey money. St. Thomas is here referring to the sin of avarice.

perfect, which means that perfection overflows from the higher to the lower part of his nature. In the imperfect beatitude of the present life, on the other hand, we proceed contrariwise from the perfection of the lower part to that of the higher part.

(394) What is most desired and willed by the intellectual nature is the supreme perfection of that nature; which perfection is its own beatitude.

(395) The rational creature naturally desires beatitude. Hence it cannot wish not to be happy.

(396) Perfect beatitude belongs naturally to God alone, as in him being and beatitude are identical. For the creature, however, beatitude is not a natural possession but is its last end.

(397) God is beatitude by his essence. . . . Men, however, only participate in beatitude; as Boethuis says, they are called "gods" by reason of some participation.

(398) Virtuous action is to be praised because it is directed towards beatitude.

(399) Virtues perfect man in actions by which he is led to beatitude.

(400) Whatever is willed is in every case directed towards beatitude, which itself is not desired on account of something else and in which the movement of the desire comes to rest.

(401) The last end and beatitude of man is his most perfect operation.

XV

**Each being naturally loves
God more than itself. (402)**

(403) Each single being is perfect in the measure in which it reaches up to its own origin.

(404) In tending towards its own perfection, everything tends towards God, for the perfections of all things are images of the divine being.

(405) The highest perfection of human life consists in the mind of man being open to God.

(406) Since the soul is created directly by God, it will not be completely happy unless it sees God directly.

(407) Every rational being knows God implicitly in every act of knowledge. For, just as nothing has the nature of desirability except through its likeness to the first goodness, so nothing is knowable except through its likeness to the first truth.

(408) The natural desire for knowledge cannot be satisfied in us until we know the first cause, and

that not in any kind of way but in its essence. God, however, is the first cause. Hence the last end of the creature endowed with a spiritual intellect is to see God in his essence.

(409) The final happiness and beatitude of any intellectual being is to know God.

(410) Purity makes the eye fit for clear vision; so also the vision of God is promised to the pure of heart.

(411) The creature is darkness compared with the excellence of the divine light. Hence created knowledge, which is derived from the power of created being, is called *evening* knowledge.

(412) Created things in themselves do not lead away from God but towards him; for *the invisible things of God are clearly seen, being understood by the things that are made* (Rom. 1.20) . But the fact that they lead us away from God arises from the fault of those who use them foolishly. Hence it is said: *creatures are made into a snare to the feet of the unwise* (Wisd. 14.11) . But even in the fact that creatures lead us away from God in this way, there is evidence that they have their being from God, for they would not be able to lead the unwise away from God

79

except by enticing them by the good which they possess from God.

(413) It is quite clearly a false opinion to say that, with regard to the truth of faith, it is completely indifferent what one thinks about created things, provided one has the right opinion about God; an error about creatures reacts in a false knowledge of God.

(414) The end and ultimate perfection of the human soul is to transcend the whole order of created things through knowledge and love, and to advance to the first cause, which is God.

(415) The end which the intellectual creature reaches by its own activity is the complete actualisation of the intellect in relation to all intelligible things lying within its capacity; in this the intellect becomes most like to God.

(415a) Although the human intellect can know only a little about divine things, yet in that knowledge it finds its desire, love and happiness more completely than in the most perfect knowledge it can have of lower things.

(416) All beings naturally strive towards God—not explicitly but implicitly.

(417) Although the soul is led to God through the intellect more than through the love of the will, yet the movement of love reaches him more perfectly than the intellect does.

(418) Man approaches nearer to God through love than through his reason, because in love man does not act himself, but is in a manner of speaking drawn nearer by God himself.

(419) Nothing lies midway between our intellect and God, either by way of efficient causality—since our minds are directly created and sanctified by God—or by way of some object causing beatitude—since the soul is beatified by enjoying God himself.

(420) Love, which is an act of the appetitive faculty, even in this life tends primarily to God and from him passes on to other things; according to this, charity loves God directly but other things through the mediation of God. In knowledge, however, the converse is true, since we know God through other things, either as cause through effects or by way of eminence or negation.

(421) It can well happen that one who is not in charity loves one created thing more than God, another equally with God and another less than

God. But it is impossible for one to love a creature equally with God and at the same time love nothing more than God, because the last end of the human will must necessarily be one single thing.

(442) Since everything is worth loving in so far as it is good, God is infinitely worth loving since his goodness is infinite. But no creature can love infinitely, since no finite power can be infinitely in act. Hence God alone can love himself in the most perfect way, since his power of loving is as great as his goodness.

(423) The reason why we are called *wayfarers* is because we are striving towards God, who is our last end and beatitude. In this life we advance by coming nearer to God, not with bodily steps but through the affection of the heart. This approach, however, is made by charity because by it the mind is united with God.

(424) Man is united with God through his will.

(425) The love of God has the power of uniting things: it reduces human affections from many to one. . . . Love of self, on the other hand, divides up human affections and diversifies them.

(426) Since every creature according to its nature

naturally belongs to God, it follows that both angel and man naturally love God more than themselves, and before themselves. Everything in its own way naturally loves God more than itself.

(427) Hope leads to love in so far as the hope of getting some good from God leads to the love of God for his own sake.

(428) All things, in so far as they have being, are like to God, who is being in the first and highest manner.

(429) It is evident that all things naturally strive after being, according to which they become like to God, who is being itself, while all other things only participate in being. Hence the last end towards which all things strive is likeness to God.

(430) All things, in so far as they have being, aim at likeness to God, who is being itself.

(431) Being is itself a likeness of the divine goodness. Hence, in so far as a thing longs for being, it desires likeness to God, and longs for God himself implicitly.

(432) The last end is the first principle of being, in which all perfection is preserved, and towards

whose likeness all things strive according to their perfection, some in relation to being only, others in relation to living being, and others in relation to living being, intelligence and beatitude.

(433) Everything which strives after its own perfection tends towards likeness to God.

(434) He who wills something under some aspect of good, has a will conformed to the divine will.

(435) All creatures participate in the divine goodness, with the result that they pour forth to others the goodness which they themselves possess. For it belongs to the nature of goodness to communicate itself to others.

(436) An inclination to good through action is implanted in every creature which comes from the hand of God. But the creature becomes more like to God by the realisation of each single good.

(437) Since God's essence and operation are identical, the highest assimilation of man to God is realised in some action. Hence beatitude, by which man is made like to God in the most complete way and which is the end of human life, consists in an action.

(438) When man omits to do what is in his power and only waits for God's help, he appears to tempt God.

(439) Since the creature endeavours to be like to God through many things, the last thing remaining to it is to seek the likeness to God, who is the cause of other things.

(440) Although there is some likeness to God in all creatures, only in the intellectual creature is this likeness by way of image . . . in other creatures it is by way of vestige or footprint.

(440a) Our likeness to God is prior to our likeness to our neighbour, which is based on the former.

(441) Creatures do not reflect their exemplar in a perfect manner. Hence they can reflect it in many ways, and there are many images. But there is only one perfect way of representation, and so there can only be one Son, who is the perfect image of the Father.

(442) There is only one perfect uncreated image. The first exemplar, the divine essence, cannot be represented perfectly by a single creature but must be represented by many created things.

(443) One result of the vision of God is the immutability of the intellect and the will. The intellect is fixed, because when the first cause in which all else can be known is reached, the quest of the spirit comes to an end. The mutability of the will also ceases, because nothing further remains to be desired when the last end, which contains in itself the plenitude of goodness, is reached.

(444) The nearer a thing is to God, who is completely immovable, the less changeable and more enduring it is.

(445) The emanation of creatures from God would be imperfect unless they returned to him in equal measure.

(446) Wood burning in a fire participates in the nature of fire; thus in a certain sense man is also made a participator in the divine nature.

(447) Since the enjoyment of God, deservedly, due to his excellence, surpasses the power of all creatures, it follows that this complete and perfect joy does not enter into man but rather man enters into it. *Enter into the joy of thy Lord* (Matt. 25.21).

XVI

Things are more in God than God is in things. (448)

(449) God himself is his own being, which can be said of no other being.

(450) Since the proper name of God is *He who is,* a nature identical with his being is proper to him alone.

(451) Since God's being cannot be as if contained in a receptacle, but is pure being, it is not limited in any determined mode of perfection of being but contains in itself the whole of being.

(452) All things in the whole world are moved to act by something else, except the first agent, whose action is such that he is in no way moved to act by anything else. In him nature and will are identical.

(453) Time has a before and after, aeon in itself has no before and after, though they can be joined

to it, but eternity has no before and after, nor does it tolerate such things.*

(454) The higher a being is, the simpler it is. Hence the beings which possess the highest degree of nobility must also possess the highest degree of simplicity.

(455) God is the first exemplar of all things.

(456) Even though all things, in so far as they exist, reflect the divine essence, yet they do not all do so in one and the same way, but in different ways and in different degrees. Thus the divine essence is the proper exemplar and idea of a particular creature in so far as it can be reflected by this determined creature in this determined way.

(457) From the one first truth there result many truths in the human mind, just as the one human face produces many images in a broken mirror.

(458) God, and what is in God, are not directed to any end but are the end.

---

* Aevum, aeviternity, or aeon is used by St. Thomas and the Scholastics to mean the measure of the duration of spiritual substances such as angels. It comes midway between time and eternity, and may be conceived as the measure of the duration of a thing which is unchangeable in itself, but whose operations involve change.

(459)   God, who acts first of all beings, does not gain anything for himself by his action, but communicates and gives out something to others. Hence things are not ordered to God as end in order to add something to him, but so that they may reach the end, each in its own way, through him who is himself the end.

(460)   God loves those who love him, but not as if their love were the reason why he loves them; rather it is the contrary.

(461)   The divine love causes the good which it loves in some thing; but it is not always so with human love.

(462)   Since God is outside the whole created order and every creature is ordered to him, but the contrary is not true, so it is clear that there is a real relation of creatures to God. There is, however, no real relation of God to creatures, but only a rational one, in so far as creatures are referred to him.

(463)   We can in truth open our hearts to God, but not without God's help.

(464)   The word perfection, if taken in its literal sense, cannot be applied to God, for nothing is made

perfect (*per-fectum*) except what is created (*factum*).

(465) We know and judge all things in the light of the first truth, for the light of our intellect, which is either natural or a gift of grace, is nothing other than an imprint of the first truth.

(466) Just as a doctor is said to cause health though he only acts exteriorly, while nature alone is active from within, so man is said to teach truth though he only announces it exteriorly while God teaches interiorly.

(467) When man teaches he only exercises an external activity like a doctor when he heals; but just as the interior nature is the principal cause of healing, so also the interior light of the mind is the principal cause of knowledge. These, however, both come from God.

(468) We acquire our interior knowledge by the fact that things impress their likeness on our souls. But in God's knowledge the contrary is true; from his mind forms flow out to all creatures. Hence, just as knowledge in us is a sealing of our souls through things, so, on the other hand, forms are nothing other than a sealing of things through God's knowledge.

(469) Human rational knowledge is in a certain sense

caused by things; hence it follows that intelligible things are the measure of human knowledge. That reality is of this nature is a true judgment of the reason, but the contrary is not true. God's mind is by its knowledge the cause of things. Hence his knowledge must necessarily be the measure of things, just as the rules of art measure the works of art, each of which is perfect in the degree in which it obeys these rules.

(470) Even if the human intellect did not exist, things would still be called true by reason of their order to the divine intellect. If, however, both intellects were thought to be no more, which is impossible, the idea of truth could not exist in any way.

(471) The knowledge of God is compared to created things as art to works of art. Hence, just as art not only knows but also creates what is artistically correct, while it only knows but does not create what deviates from the rules of art, so God's knowledge both knows and creates all good things, while it only knows sin and evil, which are deviations from his eternal law, but does not cause them.

(472) God's purpose is not frustrated in those who sin or in those who attain salvation.

(473) There remains one reason for the angels' joy, both when men repent and when they sin, namely that the order of divine providence is fulfilled.

(474) Just as a pottery vase could expect to be put to good use by the potter, so man must hope to expect right guidance from God.

(475) It is a feature of mercy that it is poured forth to others and, what is more, that it should comfort the poverty of others. But this belongs in the highest degree to the superior. Hence, mercy belongs properly to God, and it is said that his omnipotence is here most clearly shown.

(476) God's omnipotence is most manifest in clemency and mercy, for the supreme power of God is most clearly evident in the fact that he forgives sins freely. He who is bound by the law of a higher authority is not free to leave sins unpunished.

(477) Divine justice always presupposes divine mercy upon which it is based. Nothing is due to the creature except with regard to something real already existing in it beforehand; and if this latter is due to the creature, again it is with regard to something prior. Since we cannot proceed to infinity, we must necessarily arrive at

something which depends only on the goodness of the divine will, which is man's last aim and end.

(478) Nothing is due to anyone except in virtue of something which has been given to him gratuitously by God.

(479) Things are said to have been created in the beginning of time, not as if the beginning of time were the measure of creation, but because heaven and earth have been created together with time.

(480) God has created all men for beatitude.

(481) Just as the primary purpose of human law is to cause friendship between men, so the purpose of the divine law is to establish friendship between men and God.

(482) The eternal law is compared to the order of the human reason as art to a work of art.

(483) God by his power does touch created things in moving them, but he himself is not touched, for the natural power of no creature is able to penetrate to God.

(484) Irrational creatures neither participate in

human reason nor do they obey it, yet they participate in the divine reason by obeying it.

(485) Wherever God is, there he is totally. Through his undivided power he is in contact with everything.

(486) Even natural love, which dwells in all things, arises from some knowledge; this knowledge, however, does not belong to things themselves but to the founder of creation.

(487) It is true that God, who is the first cause, does not enter into the essences of created things; yet created being can only be understood as having arisen from the divine being.

(488) It is clear that all inferior beings, though they are active, do not give being to other things except in so far as the power of God acts in them.

(489) God must be in all things in the most intimate way. . . . The fact that he acts directly in all things is a sign of the almighty power of God.

(490) Everything which acts must be said to act through the power of God. It is God himself who is the cause of the activity of all things.

(491) Though created things produce their own proper effects, yet it is not superfluous that God should also produce the same effects, because the creature produces nothing except through the power of God. Nor is it superfluous that the effects which God can produce by himself should also be produced by other causes. This comes not from any insufficiency in the divine power, but from the immensity of God's goodness, through which he has wished to communicate his likeness to things—not only by giving them existence but also in making them the causes of other things. In this double way the image of God is common to all creatures. Here also is manifested the beauty of the order in creation.

(492) All creatures are nothing other than an objective expression and representation of what is contained in the concept of the divine Word.

(493) Knowledge and will mean that the thing known is in the knower and the thing willed is in the willer. Thus, according to knowledge and will, things are more in God than God is in things.

(494) We know that everything done by God dwells in him as known, so it follows that all created things are in him as in the divine life. . . . Also

the natures of inanimate things are alive in God's mind, in which they have divine existence.

(495) Since God is the universal cause of all being, it is thus necessary that wherever being is found, God is also there present.

(496) God is the cause of all action in so far as he grants the power of acting, which he preserves and brings into act, and in so far as it is through his power that every other power is active. When we realise that God is his own power and that he dwells in every being, not as part of its essence but as holding it in being, it follows that God himself must act directly in every agent; this, however, does not exclude the action of the will and of nature.

(497) The natural necessity indwelling in things which are determined to a single end is the action of God directing them to their end, just as the necessity by which an arrow is determined to fly to a certain target is an action of the archer and not of the arrow. But there is a difference; what creatures receive from God is their nature, but what man impresses on natural things, in addition to their nature, is the compulsion of force. Hence, just as the necessary compulsion in the flight of the arrow shows the aim of the archer, so the natural

necessity in creatures manifests the direction of divine providence.

(498) God moves all things in their own manner. Hence some things participate in the divine movement in a necessary way, but the rational creature is moved freely.

(499) It is not contrary to the idea of nature that natural things should be moved by God as first mover, since nature is a kind of instrument used by God. In the same way there is nothing contradictory in the idea of voluntary action arising from God, in so far as the will is moved by God.

(500) God's providence cares for all things in their own manner . . . Voluntary action, and mastery over that action, are peculiar to man and to spiritual creatures. To this compulsion is opposed. Hence God does not compel man to act rightly.

(501) God's action as first cause is perfect, but natural action is also needed as second cause. God could do what nature does without the help of nature, but it is his will to act through the medium of nature so that order may be preserved in things.

(502) God does not justify us without any action on our part.

(503) Divine providence does not destroy the nature of things but preserves it.

(504) The gifts of grace are joined to nature in such a way that they do not destroy but perfect it. Hence the light of faith, which flows into us through grace, does not extinguish the light of natural knowledge which is our natural inheritance.

(505) Grace does not destroy nature but presupposes and perfects it.

XVII

This is the final human knowledge of God: to know that we do not know God. (506)

(507) Although uncreated truth exceeds all created truth, yet there is nothing to prevent created truth from being better known to us. Things which are less known in themselves are known better by us.

(508) God is one in reality but multiple according to our minds; we know him in as many ways as created things represent him.

(509) The necessity of calling God by many names is evident. Since we cannot know God naturally except from his effects, so it is necessary to designate his perfection by different names, just as different perfections are found in created things. If, however, we were able to comprehend his essence in itself and give him a name proper to his essence, then we would express him in a single name. This is promised to those who will see God in his essence. *In that day*

there shall be one Lord, and his name shall be one. (Zach.14.9) .

(510) Created things are not sufficient to represent the creator. Hence we cannot possibly arrive at perfect knowledge of the creator from creatures; in addition, because of the weakness of our intellect we cannot even know all that created things manifest of God.

(511) God can in no way be said to be like creatures; but creatures can truly be called like to God in a certain sense.

(512) No human affections in the strict sense can actually be in God also, with the exception of joy and love.

(513) Even though a creature may be very like God, yet it never arrives at the stage when something is due to it in the way that things are due to God.

(514) From his effects we know that God exists, that he is the cause of other things, and that he excels everything else which he leaves far below him; that is the final perfection of our knowledge in this life.

(515) The truths of faith, which can only be known

completely by those who see the essence of God, can be known by the human reason only in similitudes, which are not sufficiently clear to give comprehensive knowledge of that truth as if by a demonstration or as if understood in itself. Nevertheless, it is useful for the human mind to exercise itself in such enquiries, inadequate as they are, provided there is no presump--tuous claim to complete understanding and demonstration. A little knowledge of the most sublime things, even though it is poor and insufficient, is a source of the highest joy.

(516) The human mind proceeds to the knowledge of God in three ways, although it does not arrive at knowledge of what he is but only that he is. Firstly: in so far as his creative action is known more perfectly. Secondly: in so far as he is the cause of higher effects, for since these bear his likeness in a higher way, they show forth his excellence more distinctly. Thirdly: in so far as he is known more and more as being far above all those things we see in his effects.

(517) The human intellect, which naturally acquires its knowledge from material things, is not able of itself to arrive at the point of seeing the divine substance in itself, since the latter is elevated incomparably above all material things and even above all other beings.

(518) Our intellect speaks of divine things, not according to their own mode of existence—for it cannot know them so—but according to the mode of existence found in created things.

(519) To know God in a created likeness is not to know the essence of God.

(520) Whatever is comprehended by a finite being is itself finite.

(521) The investigation of divine things in such a way as if one were able to comprehend them completely is presumptuous and is forbidden.

(522) It is impossible to predicate anything of God and of other beings in the same sense.

(523) The reason cannot track down the will of God except with regard to what he must will with absolute necessity; but his will in relation to creatures is not of such a kind.

(524) God is not called incomprehensible because there is something in him which cannot be seen, but because he is not seen as perfectly as he can be seen.

(525) God is honoured by silence, not because we may say or know nothing about him, but be-

cause we know that we are unable to comprehend him.

(526) Neither Christian nor pagan knows the nature
of God as he is in himself.

(527) In this life we cannot know perfectly what God
is, but we can know what he is not, and in this
consists the perfection of our knowledge as wayfarers in this world. Likewise, in this life we
cannot love God perfectly so that we are per-
manently turned towards him in act, but only
imperfectly so that our minds are never turned
towards what is contrary to him.

(528) The divine substance in its immensity exceeds
every form which can be grasped by our minds.
Hence we cannot comprehend it by knowing
what it is, but only have a slight knowledge of
it in knowing what it is not.

(529) We only know God truly when we believe that
he is above all that men can think about God.

(530) It is said that at the end of our knowledge God
is ultimately known as unknown, because then
the mind knows God most perfectly when it
knows that his essence is above all that can be
known in this life of wayfaring.

(531) Even though the eye of the owl does not see the sun, nevertheless the eye of the eagle gazes at it.

Key to the Abbreviations in the Index of References

In the following index of references, the references to the Summa Theologica are represented only by numbers. For example, II-II, 123, 2 means the II Part of the II part, question 123, article 2 .The same holds good for the commentary on the Books of the Sentences of Peter Lombard. For example, 3, d. 33, 2, 5, means the 3rd. Book, dist. 33, question 2, article 5. The other works are abbreviated as follows:

C.G. = Summa contra Gentiles.
Comp. theol. = Compendium theologiae.
Ver. = Questiones disputatae de veritate.
Pot. = Questiones disputatae de potentia Dei.
Mal. = Questiones disputatae de malo.
Car. = Questiones disputatae de caritate.
Corr. frat. = Questiones disputatae de corr. fraterna.
De spe = Questiones disputatae de spe.
Virt. comm. = Questiones disputatae de virtutibus in communi.
Virt. card. = Questiones disputatae de virtutibus cardinalibus.
Spir. creat. = Questiones disputatae de spiritualibus creaturis.
An. = Questiones disputatae de anima.
Quol. = Questiones quodlibetales.
Perf. vit. spir. = De perfectione vitae spiritualis.
Nat. verb. = De natura verbi intellectus.
Un. int. = De unitate intellectus contra Averoistas.
Comm. in An. = Commentary on Aristotle's De anima.
In Met. = Commentary on the Metaphysics of Aristotle.
In Joh. = Commentary on the Gospel of St. John.
In Matth. = Commentary on the Gospel of St. Matthew.
In Trin. = Commentary on Boethius on the Trinity.
In div. nom. = Commentary on Pseudo-Dionysius on the Divine Names.
Praec. car. = De duobus praeceptis caritatis.

Index of References

(1) Pot. 7, 9.
(2) C.G. 1, 83.

(3) Pot. 3, 16 ad 1.
(4) C.G. 1, 102.

(5) C.G. 4, 11.
(6) I-II, 16, 4.
(7) C.G. 1, 28.
(8) I-II, 1, 6.
(9) C.G. 3, 90.
(10) C.G. 3, 24.
(11) C.G. 2, 6.
(12) I-II, 111, 1.
(13) C.G. 2, 46.
(14) Ver. 24, 1 ad 16.
(15) Ver. 5, 3 ad 3.
(16) C.G. 3, 136.
(17) I, 84, 1 ad 3.
(18) Ver. 16, 2.
(19) C.G. 3, 74.
(20) Comp. theol. I, 148.
(21) C.G. 2, 68.
(22) C.G. 1, 1.
(23) Car. 1 ad 11.
(24) I, 65, 1 ad 1.
(25) Ver. 18, 2 ad 5.
(26) I, 104, 3 ad 1.
(27) C.G. 2, 30.
(28) Pot. 5, 1 ad 16.
(29) Ver. 24, 8 ad 14.
(30) Ver. 22, 6 ad 3.
(31) 2, d. 23, 1.
(32) C.G. 2, 30.
(33) I, 103, 1 ad 2.
(34) I, 104, 1 ad 1.
(35) I, 104, 3 ad 3.
(36) I, 109, 1 ad 1.
(37) Ver. 20, 4.
(38) C.G. 3, 7.
(39) Ver. 21, 3.
(40) I-II, 29, 5.
(41) Ver. 16, 3 ad 5.
(42) C.G. 3, 7.
(43) Pot. 3, 16 ad 3.
(44) I, 5, 3 ad 2.
(45) Ver. 8, 4 ad 5.
(46) Pot. 3, 6 ad 20.
(47) C.G. 2, 89.
(48) I, 8, 1 ad 4.
(49) I, 63, 4.
(50) Mal. 1, 1.

(51) Comp. theol. I, 114.
(52) I-II, 19, 7 ad 3.
(53) I-II, 20, 2.
(54) C.G. 1, 28.
(55) C.G. 1, 37.
(56) Ver. 21, 3 ad 2.
(57) I, 6, 3 ad 2.
(58) I-II, 36, 3.
(59) I-II, 8, 1.
(60) I-II, 78, 1 ad 2.
(61) C.G. 4, 92.
(62) I, 19, 9.
(63) Pot. 3, 6 ad 14.
(64) C.G. 3, 4.
(65) I-II, 6, 4 ad 3.
(66) I-II, 27, 1 ad 1.
(67) Ver. 22, 6.
(68) I-II, 35, 1 ad 3.
(69) I-II, 29, 3 ad 2.
(70) Mal. 1, 4.
(71) I, 48, 5; I, 48, 6.
(72) I-II, 79, 1 ad 4.
(73) Mal. 1, 5 ad 10.
(74) I, 49, 2.
(75) I, 63, 8.
(76) Corr. frat. 1 ad 4.
(77) Mal. 10, 1 ad 5.
(78) Mal. 1, 3.
(79) C.G. 3, 10.
(80) C.G. 3, 11.
(81) I, 17, 4 ad 2.
(82) Mal. 12, 1 ad 10.
(83) C.G. 3, 9.
(84) C.G. 3, 12; cf. I, 48, 4.
(85) C.G. 3, 71.
(86) Ver. 16, 2 (sed contra).
(87) I, 49, 3.
(88) Comp. theol. I, 117.
(89) I, 103, 7 ad 1.
(90) Ver. 24, 10 ad 11.
(91) Ver. 22, 6 ad 6.
(92) Mal. 2, 12.
(93) Ver. 5, 4 ad 6.
(94) Comp. theol. I, 142.
(95) I, 48, 2 ad 3.
(96) I, 92, 1 ad 3.

(97) C.G. 3, 71.
(98) C.G. 3, 112.
(99) C.G. 3, 112.
(100) C.G. 3, 22.
(101) C.G. 1, 43.
(102) C.G. 3, 112.
(103) I-II, 32, 2.
(104) Comm. in An. 3, 8, lect. 13.
(105) Ver. 20, 3; Ver. 20, 3 ad 5.
(106) Ver. 2, 2.
(107) C.G. 3, 113.
(108) I, 75, 4.
(109) I, 76, 7 ad 3.
(110) Un. int.
(111) Spir. creat. 2 ad 5.
(112) Ver. 13, 3 ad 2.
(113) I, 85, 7.
(114) An. 8.
(115) I, 76, 5.
(116) C.G. 3, 81.
(117) I, 77, 2.
(118) Virt. comm. 9.
(119) An. 13.
(120) Mal. 16, 8 ad 7.
(121) I-II, 31, 4 ad 3.
(122) C.G. 1, 43.
(123) Mal. 9, 1.
(124) C.G. 3, 59.
(125) I-II, 32, 8.
(126) C.G. 1, 43.
(127) C.G. 1, 5.
(128) In div. nom. 4, 4.
(129) I, 14, 1.
(130) Ver. 1, 9.
(131) Ver. 2, 2 ad 2.
(132) I, 84, 7.
(133) I, 12, 12.
(134) Ver. 12, 3 ad 2.
(135) Ver. 18, 2 ad 7.
(136) In Trin. 6, 3.
(137) I, 85, 6.
(138) Ver. 1, 9.
(139) C.G. 2, 66.
(140) Ver. 24, 2.
(141) Ver. 25, 1.
(142) De spe 1 ad 7.
(142a) II-II, 26, 1 ad 2.
(143) I-II, 93, 1 ad 3.
(144) I, 14, 8 ad 3.
(145) Nat. verb.
(146) Ver. 10, 8.
(147) I, 84, 5.
(148) Ver. 16, 1 (sed contra).
(149) Ver. 22, 10.
(150) I, 108, 6 ad 3.
(151) I, 82, 3.
(152) I-II, 28, 1 ad 3.
(153) I-II, 26, 2 ad 2.
(154) I-II, 86, 1 ad 2.
(155) C.G. 1, 77; cf. I, 16, 1; Ver. 26, 3.
(156) Mal. 6, 1 ad 13.
(157) I, 79, 11 ad 2.
(158) I, 59, 2 ad 3.
(159) C.G. 1, 71.
(160) C.G. 3, 26.
(161) I-II, 19, 3 ad 1.
(162) Car. 3, ad 12.
(163) I-II, 4, 4 ad 2.
(164) Ver. 23, 6.
(165) Ver. 24, 10 ad 15.
(166) Ver. 21, 3.
(167) II-II, 27, 4, obj. 1 ad 1.
(168) I-II, 5 ad 2.
(169) Ver. 25, 1.
(170) I-II, 27, 1.
(171) I-II, 28, 6.
(172) De spe 3.
(173) I, 20, 1.
(174) I-II, 55, 1 ad 4.
(175) I-II, 17, 5 ad 3.
(176) Corr. frat. 1, ad 5.
(177) I-II, 26, 1 ad 3.
(178) Car. 1.
(179) I, 60, 1 ad 3.
(180) Ver. 22, 5.
(181) C.G. 3, 26.
(182) I, 60, 5.
(183) II-II, 154, 12.
(184) C.G. 1, 7.
(185) Mal. 2, 3 ad 2.
(186) I-II, 17, 9 ad 2.

(187) II-II, 50, 4.
(188) C.G. 2, 79.
(189) Ver. 16, 2 ad 5.
(190) I-II, 58, 1 ad 3.
(191) II-II, 154, 12, ad 1.
(192) C.G. 3, 126.
(193) I, 98, 1.
(194) In Joh. 1, 7.
(195) II-II, 130, 1.
(196) II-II, 133, 1; II-II, 142, 1.
(197) I, 63, 9.
(198) Quol. 3, 22.
(199) II-II, 108, 2.
(200) I-II, 58, 4 ad 3.
(201) I-II, 71, 2 ad 1.
(202) Virt. comm. 8, ad 17.
(203) I-II, 58, 4 ad 3.
(204) Virt. comm. 8 ad 10.
(205) Mal. 8, 2.
(206) Mal. 14, 2 ad 8.
(207) II-II, 145, 3.
(208) Virt. comm. 9.
(209) I-II, 71, 6.
(210) C.G. 4, 70.
(211) I-II, 59, 4.
(212) II-II, 155, 1 ad 2.
(213) II-II, 153, 3.
(214) Virt. comm. 12 ad 16; II-II, 157, 2.
(215) Virt. comm. 8.
(216) C.G. 1, 71.
(217) I-II, 66, 1; Virt. comm. 4 ad 3.
(218) II-II, 47, 6.
(219) I-II, 58, 2.
(220) II-II, 20, 1.
(221) II-II, 145, 2.
(222) I-II, 19, 5.
(223) Ver. 17, 3 ad 3.
(224) I-II, 19, 5 ad 2.
(225) Ver. 17, 1 ad 1.
(226) Ver. 17, 3 ad 1.
(227) Ver. 17, 5.
(228) I, 82, 1 ad 3.
(229) I, 59, 3.
(230) Mal. 6, 1 ad 22.

(231) Ver. 24, 3 ad 2.
(232) I, 82, 1 ad 3.
(233) Ver. 22, 6.
(234) I, 83, 2.
(235) II-II, 29, 2.
(236) Ver. 22, 1 ad 12.
(237) I-II, 18, 7 ad 2.
(238) I-II, 1, 6.
(239) Virt. comm. 7 ad 2.
(240) I, 5, 4 ad 3.
(241) Virt. comm. 9 ad 16.
(242) Mal. 1, 5.
(243) I-II, 19, 8 ad 2.
(244) I-II, 90, 1 ad 3.
(245) I-II, 8, 3 ad 2.
(246) Virt. comm. 5 ad 8.
(247) Praec. car. (princ).
(248) C.G. 1, 88.
(249) I-II, 14, 2.
(250) C.G. 1, 1.
(251) C.G. 1, 1.
(252) I-II, 77, 2 ad 1.
(253) I-II, 66, 5 ad 1.
(254) I-II, 66, 5 ad 2.
(255) C.G. 1, 2.
(256) C.G. 1, 2.
(257) I-II, 56, 2 ad 2.
(258) Ver. 18, 7 ad 7.
(259) II-II, 51, 1 ad 2.
(260) Virt. comm. 5 ad 8.
(261) Perf. vit. spir. 23.
(262) Quol. 1, 14.
(263) II-II, 32, 3.
(264) II-II, 182, 1 ad 3.
(265) Virt. comm. 6.
(266) Car. 3 ad 13.
(267) II-II, 56, 2 ad 3.
(268) Ver. 14, 6.
(269) II-II, 47, 2 ad 1.
(270) Virt. comm. 12 ad 23.
(271) II-II, 119, 3 ad 3; II-II, 55, 2 ad 3.
(272) II-II, 47, 5 ad 2.
(273) Virt. comm. 6 ad 2.
(274) II-II, 49, 3 ad 3.
(275) II-II, 47, 14 ad 2.

(276) II-II, 50, 1.
(277) Virt. card. 2 ad 4.
(278) I-II, 73, 1 ad 2.
(279) II-II, 153, 5 ad 1.
(280) I-II, 59, 2 (sed contra).
(281) I-II, 59, 1.
(282) I-II, 59, 5 ad 3.
(283) Mal. 12, 1.
(284) Ver. 26, 7 ad 1.
(285) II-II, 158, 1 ad 2.
(286) II-II, 125, 1 ad 1.
(287) Ver. 26, 5.
(288) C.G. 1, 89.
(289) I-II, 37, 4.
(290) Virt. comm. 12 ad 9.
(291) Mal. 12, 1 ad 4.
(292) II-II, 158, 8 ad 2.
(293) I-II, 46, 6 ad 1.
(294) I-II, 40, 4 ad 3.
(295) I-II, 67, 4 ad 2.
(296) I-II, 43, 1 (sed contra).
(297) I-II, 44, 2 ad 3.
(298) Virt. comm. 11 ad 15.
(299) Mal. 7, 1.
(300) I-II, 77, 4.
(301) C.G. 4, 70.
(302) II-II, 125, 2.
(303) I-II, 73, 5.
(304) I-II, 1, 7 ad 1.
(305) I-II, 18, 5.
(306) I-II, 109, 2 ad 2.
(307) Virt. comm. 9 ad 15; Virt. card. 3.
(308) II-II, 123, 4.
(309) C.G. 1, 90.
(310) I-II, 2, 6 ad 3.
(311) I-II, 34, 1 ad 2.
(312) C.G. 1, 90.
(313) Mal. 10, 3.
(314) I-II, 32, 8 ad 3.
(315) I-II, 31, 6.
(316) I-II, 34, 4 ad 2.
(317) I-II, 2, 6 ad 1; I-II, 34, 2 ad 3.
(318) C.G. 1, 90.
(319) I-II, 34, 3 ad 3.

(320) I-II, 35, 5.
(321) I-II, 39, 4 ad 1.
(322) II-II, 31, 3.
(323) II-II, 23, 6 ad 1.
(324) II-II, 23, 7.
(325) Ver. 10, 10 ad 7.
(326) Car. 8 ad 11, ad 12.
(327) Car. 8 ad 17.
(328) II-II, 27, 8 ad 3.
(329) II-II, 123, 12 ad 2.
(330) C.G. 3, 28.
(331) II-II, 29, 1; II-II, 29, 1 ad 3.
(331a) II-II, 45, 6 ad 1.
(332) I, 96, 3 ad 2.
(333) Car. 9 ad 18.
(334) II-II, 124, 5 ad 3.
(335) I-II, 92, 1 ad 3.
(336) II-II, 141, 8.
(337) I-II, 113, 9 ad 2.
(338) I-II, 2, 4 ad 2.
(339) I-II, 2, 4 ad 1.
(340) I-II, 96, 6.
(341) I-II, 99, 5 ad 1.
(342) I-II, 100, 9.
(343) I-II, 100, 2.
(344) I-II, 65, 4.
(345) In Matth. 5, 1.
(346) I, 21, 3 ad 2.
(347) II-II, 30, 2.
(348) II-II, 55, 8.
(349) II-II, 124, 1.
(350) II-II, 123, 12 ad 3.
(351) II-II, 124, 3.
(352) II-II, 131, 1 ad 3.
(353) II-II, 126, 1.
(354) II-II, 123, 12 ad 2.
(355) I-II, 45, 3.
(356) C.G. 3, 34.
(357) II-II, 128, 1.
(358) II-II, 123, 6.
(359) II-II, 123, 6 ad 2.
(360) II-II, 123, 6 ad 1.
(361) I-II, 66, 4 ad 2.
(362) Virt. card. 1, 1 ad 14.
(363) II-II, 136, 4 ad 2.
(364) II-II, 143.

(365) II-II, 151, 4 ad 2.
(366) II-II, 142, 4.
(367) II II, 146, 1 ad 4.
(368) I-II, 108, 3 ad 4.
(369) II-II, 142, 1 ad 2.
(370) II-II, 150, 1 ad 1.
(371) II-II, 150, 1 ad 1.
(372) II-II, 53, 6 ad 2.
(373) II-II, 180, 2 ad 3.
(374) Ver. 25, 2.
(375) Ver. 25, 6 ad 4; Mal. 12, 4.
(376) II-II, 157, 4.
(377) Mal. 8, 2 ad 1.
(378) II-II, 162, 6 ad 3; Ver. 25, 7 ad 5.
(379) II-II, 162, 5 ad 3.
(380) II-II, 161, 5 ad 4.
(381) In Matth. 11.
(382) Mal. 8. 3 ad 8.
(383) II-II, 161, 3.
(384) II-II, 133, 1 ad 3.
(385) II-II, 55, 8 ad 2.
(386) II-II, 36, 1 ad 2.
(387) I-II, 7, 2.
(388) I-II, 69, 1.
(389) III, 15, 10.
(390) I-II, 5, 8.
(391) C.G. 3, 27.
(392) Mal. 13, 3 ad 2.
(393) I-II, 3, 3 ad 3.
(394) C.G. 1, 100.
(395) C.G. 4, 92.
(396) I, 62, 4.
(397) I-II, 3, 1 ad 1.
(398) C.G. 3, 27; I-II, 13, 3 ad 1.
(399) I-II, 62, 1.
(400) C.G. 1, 101.
(401) C.G. 3, 28.
(402) I, 60, 5 ad 1.
(403) I, 12, 1.
(404) I, 6, 1 ad 2.
(405) C.G. 3, 130.
(406) Quol. 10, 17.
(407) Ver. 22, 2 ad 1.
(408) Comp. theol. I, 104.
(409) C.G. 3, 25.

(410) I-II, 69, 4.
(411) I, 64, 1 ad 3.
(412) I, 65, 1 ad 3.
(413) C.G. 2, 3.
(414) C.G. 2, 87.
(415) Comp. theol. I, 103.
(415a) C.G. 3, 25.
(416) Ver. 22, 2.
(417) Ver. 22, 11 ad 10.
(418) I-II, 26, 3 ad 4.
(419) Ver. 27, 1 ad 10.
(420) II-II, 27, 4.
(421) Mal. 7, 1 ad 20.
(422) Perf. vit. spir. 3.
(423) II-II, 24, 4.
(424) I-II, 87, 6.
(425) I-II, 73, 1 ad 3.
(426) I, 60, 5; I, 60, 5 ad 1.
(427) De spe 3.
(428) C.G. 1, 80.
(429) C.G. 3, 19.
(430) II-II, 34, 1 ad 3.
(431) Ver. 22, 2 ad 2.
(432) I-II, 2, 5 ad 3.
(433) C.G. 3, 21.
(434) I-II, 19, 10 ad 1.
(435) I, 106, 4.
(436) Ver. 20, 4.
(437) I-II, 55, 2 ad 3.
(438) II-II, 53, 4 ad 1.
(439) C.G. 3, 21.
(440) I, 93, 6.
(440a) II-II, 26, 2 ad 2.
(441) Pot. 3, 16 ad 12.
(442) I, 47, 1 ad 2.
(443) Comp. theol. I, 149.
(444) C.G. 3, 62.
(445) Ver. 20, 4.
(446) I-II, 62, 1 ad 1.
(447) II-II, 28, 3.
(448) I, 8, 3 ad 3.
(449) Spir. creat. 1.
(450) C.G. 2, 52; I, 13, 11.
(451) Pot. 1, 2.
(452) I, 60, 1 ad 2.
(453) I, 10, 5.

(454) C.G. 1, 18.
(455) I, 44, 3.
(456) Quol. 4, 1.
(457) Quol. 10, 7.
(458) Pot. 1, 2 ad 1.
(459) C.G. 3, 18.
(460) Ver. 27, 2 ad 1.
(461) C.G. 3, 150.
(462) I, 13, 7.
(463) Ver. 24, 15 ad 2.
(464) Ver. 2, 3 ad 13.
(465) I, 88, 3 ad 1.
(466) Ver. 11, 1 ad 7.
(467) I, 117, 1 ad 1.
(468) Ver. 2, 1 ad 6.
(469) C.G. 1, 61.
(470) Ver. 1, 2.
(471) Quol. 5, 2.
(472) I, 63, 7 ad 2.
(473) I, 113, 7 ad 3.
(474) Comp. theol. 2, 4.
(475) II-II, 30, 4.
(476) I, 25, 3 ad 3.
(477) I, 21, 4.
(478) I, 25, 3 ad 3.
(479) I, 46, 3 ad 1.
(480) Ver. 23, 2.
(481) I-II, 99, 2.
(482) I-II, 71, 2 ad 4.
(483) I, 105, 2 ad 1.
(484) I-II, 93, 5 ad 2.
(485) C.G. 3, 68.
(486) I-II, 27, 2 ad 3.
(487) Pot. 3, 5 ad 1.
(488) C.G. 3, 66.
(489) I, 8, 1; I, 8, 1 ad 3.
(490) C.G. 3, 67.
(491) C.G. 3, 70.
(492) C.G. 4, 42.
(493) I, 8, 3 ad 3.

(494) I, 18, 4; I, 18, 4 ad 2.
(495) C.G. 3, 68.
(496) Pot. 3, 7.
(497) I, 103, 1 ad 3.
(498) Quol. 1, 7 ad 2.
(499) I-II, 6, 1 ad 3.
(500) C.G. 3, 148.
(501) Pot. 3, 7 ad 16.
(502) I-II, 111, 2 ad 2.
(503) I-II, 10, 4.
(504) In Trin. 2, 3.
(505) Ver. 14, 10 ad 9; I, 1, 8 ad 2; I, 2, 2 ad 1.
(506) Pot. 7, 5 ad 14.
(507) Ver. 10, 12 ad 6.
(508) I, 13, 4 ad 3.
(509) C.G. 1, 31.
(510) Ver. 5, 2 ad 11.
(511) Ver. 2, 11 ad 1.
(512) C.G. 1, 91.
(513) Ver. 2, 11.
(514) C.G. 3, 49.
(515) C.G. 1, 8.
(516) In Trin. 1, 2.
(517) C.G. 4, 1.
(518) I, 39, 2.
(519) I, 12, 4 ad 1.
(520) I-II, 4, 3 ad 1.
(521) In Trin. 2, 1 ad 2.
(522) C.G. 1, 32.
(523) I, 46, 2.
(524) I, 12, 7 ad 2.
(525) In Trin. 2, 1 ad 6.
(526) I, 13, 10 ad 5.
(527) Car. 10, ad 2 (contra).
(528) C.G. 1, 14; I, 3 (prooemium).
(529) C.G. 1, 5; Ver. 8, 1 ad 8.
(530) In Trin. 1, 2 ad 1.
(531) In Joh. prologus.

Printed in the USA
CPSIA information can be obtained
at www.ICGtesting.com
LVHW091812141124
796564LV00001B/54